WHAT IS A
DEMOCRACY?

SUSAN BRIGHT-MOORE

Crabtree Publishing Company
www.crabtreebooks.com

Crabtree Publishing Company
www.crabtreebooks.com

Produced and developed by Netscribes Inc.

Author: Susan Bright-Moore
Publishing plan research and development:
  Sean Charlebois, Reagan Miller
  Crabtree Publishing Company
Editors: Valerie J. Weber, Lynn Peppas
Proofreaders: Sarah Chasse, Wendy Scavuzzo
Art director: Dibakar Acharjee
Picture researcher: Sandeep Kumar Guthikonda
Print coordinator: Katherine Berti
Project coordinator: Kathy Middleton
Production coordinator: Kenneth J. Wright
Prepress technician: Kenneth J. Wright
Cover design: Margaret Amy Salter and Katherine Berti

Front cover: President Obama is the 44th elected president of the United States of America. (right); Officials in the United States are elected using a private ballot system. (background); Ostraka voting tokens from Ancient Greece (bottom left and middle)
Title page: The White House in Washington D.C.

Photographs:
Title page: Vacclav/Shutterstock; P4: adoc-photos/Corbis; P5: AP Photo/The Canadian Press, Michelle Siu; P6: Volina/Shutterstock; P7: Porterfield – Chickering/Photo Researchers/Gettyimages; P8-9: Mart/Shutterstock; P10:Gjon Mili//Time Life Pictures/Getty Images; P11: Volina/Shutterstock; P12: Photos.com/Thinkstock; P13: BLUE LANTERN STUDIO / LAUGHING E/Blue Lantern Studio/Corbis; P14: Bettmann/CORBIS; P15: ADEM ALTAN/AFP/GettyImages; P16: House of Lords 2012/Roger Harris/UK Parliament via flickr; P17: Brooks Kraft/Corbis; P18.1: Eric Engman/ZUMA Press/Corbis; P18.2: Paul Hakimata Photography / Shutterstock.com; P19: Tan Kian Khoon/Shutterstock; P20: Brett Marty/Corbis; P21: Nirot Sriprasit/123RF; P22: Alex Wong/Getty Images; P23: Chip Somodevilla/Getty Images; P24: Stockbyte/Thinkstock; P25.1: Bettmann/CORBIS; P25.2: Antoine Serra/Sygma/Corbis; P26: WISSAM SALEH/AFP/GettyImages; P27: RHONA WISE/AFP/Getty Images; P28: Matthias Kulka/Corbis; P29: Brendan Hoffman/Getty Images; P30: Daniel Acker/Bloomberg via Getty Images; P31: Foto24/Gallo Images/Getty Images; P32: PETER MUHLY/AFP/Getty Images; P33: UK Parliament; P34: Mark Makela/Corbis; P35: GEOFF ROBINS/AFP/Getty Images; P36: Lizette Potgieter/Shutterstock; P37: bloomua/Shutterstock; P40: Visions of America/UIG via Getty Images; P41: Olivier Douliery/Pool via Bloomberg; P42: Mike Flippo/Shutterstock; P43: L. Kragt Bakker/ Shutterstock; P44: justasc/Shutterstock; P45: Jim Barber/Shutterstock. Wikimedia Commons/Marsyas: front cover (round voting chips); Wikimedia Commons/Tilemahos Efthimiadas: front cover (black pottery chips); Wikimedia Commons/Pete Souza: front cover (right); Shutterstock: front cover (background)

Library and Archives Canada Cataloguing in Publication

Bright-Moore, Susan
    What is a democracy? / Sue Bright-Moore.

(Forms of government)
Includes index.
Issued also in electronic format.
ISBN 978-0-7787-5316-2 (bound).--ISBN 978-0-7787-5323-0 (pbk.)

    1. Democracy--Juvenile literature. I. Title. II. Series: Forms of government (St. Catharines, Ont.)

JC423.B75 2013   j321.8   C2013-901025-4

Library of Congress Cataloging-in-Publication Data

Bright-Moore, Susan
    What is a democracy / Sue Bright-Moore.
        pages cm. -- (Forms of government)
    Includes index.
    ISBN 978-0-7787-5316-2 (reinforced library binding) --
ISBN 978-0-7787-5323-0 (pbk.) -- ISBN 978-1-4271-8787-1
(electronic pdf) -- ISBN 978-1-4271-9625-5 (electronic html)
    1. Democracy--Juvenile literature. I. Title.

JC423.B7843 2013
321.8--dc23
                                        2013004910

Crabtree Publishing Company
www.crabtreebooks.com   1-800-387-7650

Printed in the U.S.A./042013/SX20130306

Published in Canada
Crabtree Publishing
616 Welland Ave.
St. Catharines, Ontario
L2M 5V6

Published in the United States
Crabtree Publishing
PMB 59051
350 Fifth Avenue, 59th Floor
New York, New York 10118

Published in the
United Kingdom
Crabtree Publishing
Maritime House
Basin Road North, Hove
BN41 1WR

Published in Australia
Crabtree Publishing
3 Charles Street
Coburg North
VIC 3058

CONTENTS

Rules and Government

What would happen if a country had no rules? People live and work with other people. Rules help them get along. It is hard to think about life without these rules. Governments decide what behavior is acceptable. They put the rules into laws. They hope to keep a country running smoothly for groups and for individuals.

Governments can take different forms. Sometimes, one person leads a government. More often, many people are in charge, and they take different roles. Small governments may be in charge of a city, town, or tribe. Larger governments may run states, provinces, or countries.

The Core of Democracy

U.S. President Abraham Lincoln once said that a democracy was a "government of the people, by the people, and for the people." The power for governing comes from the people. In a democracy, people elect their own leaders. These leaders are expected to represent the people, their ideas, and their interests.

Concerns of Democracies

Inclusivity Power is in the hands of the people in a democracy. They act directly or through their leaders. Every person can **participate** and express an opinion.

Mahatma Gandhi was a leader who brought democracy to India. He overcame the rule of Great Britain through nonviolent protest.

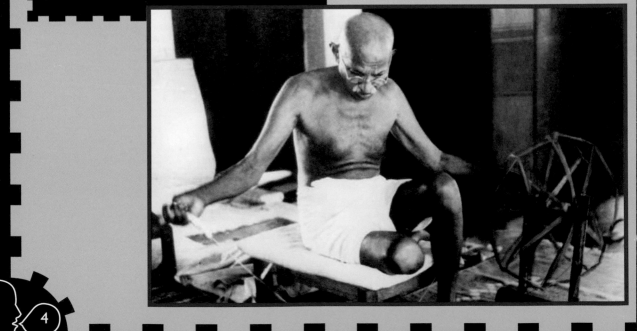

ASSEMBLY OF FIRST NATIONS
33RD ANNUAL GENERAL ASSEMBLY

ASSEMBLÉE DES PREMIÈRES NATIONS
33 ASSEMBLÉE GÉNÉRALE ANNUELLE

"HONOURING OUR TRADITIONS

HONORER NOS TRADITIONS - Agir pour notre avenir

The Assembly of First Nations is a group of First Nations chiefs in Canada today.

Human Rights In a democracy, the government respects people's freedom of speech. People have the right to gather to talk about issues. They can express their opinions without fear of punishment.

Free Elections People of voting age may vote in free and fair elections.

Compromise and Majority Rule People must work together to gain **consensus**. They must listen to and respect different viewpoints.

Democracies are often organized with three branches of government: the executive, the legislative, and the judicial. The legislative branch makes the laws. The executive branch puts the laws to work. The judicial branch makes sure that the laws are followed. The purpose of having the three branches is to separate the powers. No single group can become too powerful. However, the branches can share their duties.

Taking the Lead

The earliest leaders in North America were shamans and chiefs. Shamans often ruled Native American or First Nations tribes. They were the spiritual leaders. They danced and chanted, hoping to bring good luck to their people.

Chiefs were local leaders. They were responsible for the people in their group. They sometimes worked with a council of elders or other groups. Some groups, such as the Zulus in South Africa, still have chiefs.

DEMOCRACY IN ACTION

The word *democracy* comes from the Greek words *demos*, meaning "people," and *kratos*, meaning "rule." It means "rule by the people."

Switzerland's people participate in their own rule. In 1847, the Swiss wrote a **constitution.** The constitution explained how the democracy would be run. The Swiss formed a national government and 26 regional groups called cantons. Elected leaders in the government make some of the decisions. Many other decisions are made directly by the people.

Swiss National Government

Switzerland's national government deals with issues relating to the whole country. It is in charge of the military and railways. It prints money. It decides how to work with other countries. The cantons make decisions about matters relating to their area. For example, decisions about schools happen in the cantons.

A president and **parliament** make up the national government. The president has a very small role. Every year, a different leader is chosen to serve as president. The leaders are picked from the seven people who are in charge of the different departments in the executive branch. The parliament is elected from the different cantons and **communes**. It makes the laws. Parliament consists of the National Council and the Council of States.

Switzerland has a direct democracy.

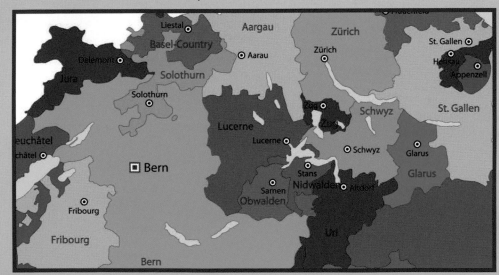

Making New Laws

Switzerland is unique. Its citizens have many chances to make decisions. In fact, the Swiss have more chances than most other countries' citizens. The decisions are made by a special kind of voting called a referendum or initiative.

A referendum is a suggestion for a new law or a change to a law or budget. Imagine that a group of people wants to make a law about guns. They could find other people who think their law is a good idea. Referendums may be called if 50,000 or more citizens ask for them. If 50,000 people agree, then the referendum is voted on. Referendums are rare in other countries.

Initiatives are ideas for changes to the constitution. If 100,000 people ask for changes, members of parliament discuss these ideas. They may take a survey to see what others think. Then they propose any changes they feel are important. If the people are not pleased, they can issue a referendum to request changes.

The Swiss national government takes a smaller role in running the country, and the regional cantons and communes take a larger role.

Communal

Imagine gathering your whole city in a building to discuss and pass laws. That still happens in some places in Switzerland. In about 2,500 small Swiss villages, all of the people meet together. They listen to ideas. They debate and discuss ideas. Then they vote to make the decision for that village.

WHERE ARE DEMOCRACIES?

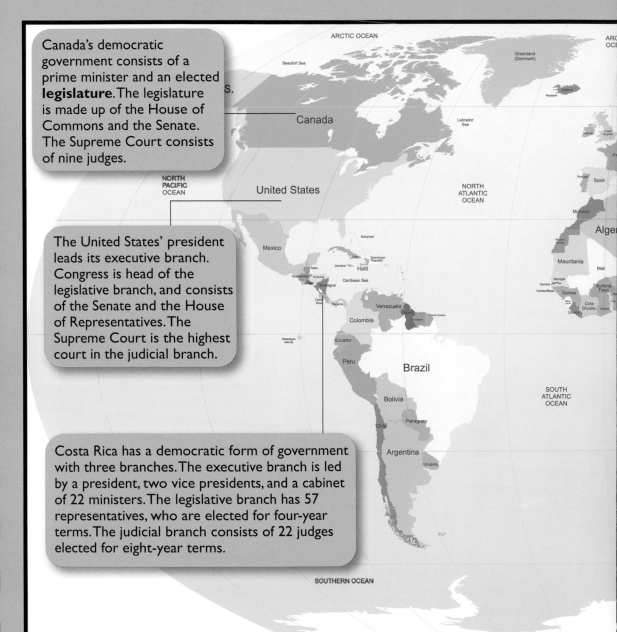

Canada's democratic government consists of a prime minister and an elected **legislature**. The legislature is made up of the House of Commons and the Senate. The Supreme Court consists of nine judges.

The United States' president leads its executive branch. Congress is head of the legislative branch, and consists of the Senate and the House of Representatives. The Supreme Court is the highest court in the judicial branch.

Costa Rica has a democratic form of government with three branches. The executive branch is led by a president, two vice presidents, and a cabinet of 22 ministers. The legislative branch has 57 representatives, who are elected for four-year terms. The judicial branch consists of 22 judges elected for eight-year terms.

A president leads India's executive branch and chooses the prime minister. However, the prime minister has more power than the president. The legislative branch is represented by a parliament with two **chambers**. The judicial branch has a supreme court and high courts.

In South Africa, the executive branch is headed by the president. He or she is elected from parliament. The legislative branch consists of the National Council of Provinces and the National Assembly. The judicial branch consists of a Constitutional Court, a Supreme Court of Appeal, and the High Court.

First Democracies

Many people believe that democracies were one of the earliest forms of government. People in a tribe or small group met to talk. They discussed their shared problems. They worked together to find answers. Written records show that, as people settled in an area, some people became wealthy and others became poorer. This change led to unequal power. Other forms of government, such as monarchies, became more common.

Athens: An Early Democracy

One of the earlier recorded democracies was in Athens, Greece, in 510 BCE. At that time, Athens had an assembly. People met on a hill near the city. Every free male over the age of 18 was allowed to vote by raising his hand. The assembly's power was limited. The Council of Five Hundred decided on an **agenda**. This council was made up of people from the surrounding area. They were chosen by a **lottery**.

Long ago, citizens of Athens crowded on Pnyx hill to listen to speakers and vote. The democratic system was in place in Athens until 411 BCE when an **oligarchy** was formed after a war.

Choosing Leaders

In early democracies, all of the people who were allowed to vote could gather. However, as the areas grew, it became more difficult for people to meet and discuss everything. The solution was to choose leaders to vote for them on smaller issues. They could then gather and vote all together on the larger, more important issues.

510 BCE–322 BCE	Ancient Greece was a democracy
500 BCE–27 BCE	Ancient Rome was a republic

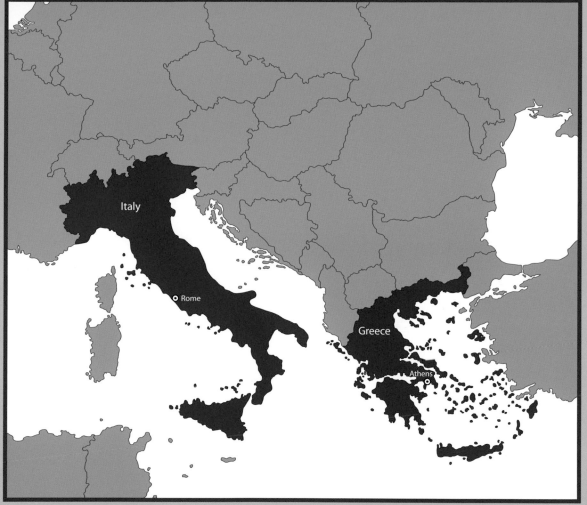

Athens and Rome, shown above on a present-day map, developed different kinds of democracies in southern Europe.

In Rome

Around the same time, the city of Rome was using a democratic government. The Roman system was called a republic.

For many years, assemblies in different cities met in a small area called the forum. They continued this practice even when the Roman Empire grew. However, the distance meant very few people were actually present. Although there were citizens who could vote, their voices were often not heard.

The Roman system was complex. It consisted of a powerful senate and four smaller assemblies, called comitia. One comitia was made up of local groups. One was made up of military units. Another was chosen from the common people. Still another was open to all citizens. When the assembly met, the votes were counted by units. The majority of the units, not the people, had to vote for an idea before it became law.

Around 800 CE, local assemblies began to appear around Europe. Local citizens gathered to talk about problems. These later meetings grew to represent larger areas. At these larger assemblies, people were often elected to represent the wishes of the people from their home area.

Parliament Evolves

The British Parliament began as a group called by the king to hear people's complaints and to serve as a court. Over time, this gathering grew into a group of leaders, called the parliament. The parliament began to handle other matters, such as taxes. By the end of the 1400s, this group began to look and act like a legislature. They began to write bills to be approved by the king.

The parliament did allow for some people's voices to be heard. But it was not a democracy. A monarch still ruled the area. It was not until 1707 that a constitution was written and Parliament gained more power.

Reform Act of 1832

Before the Reform Act of 1832, only men over the age of 20 who owned property were allowed to vote in Britain. Only about five percent of the population could vote. The Reform Act of 1832 extended the number of people who could vote. The act continued to be changed in 1867, 1884, and 1918 to remove restrictions on male voters. In 1928, it was extended to include women.

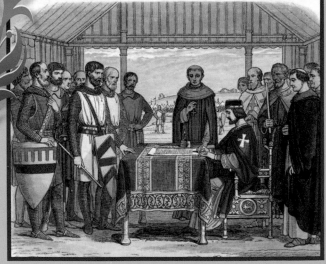

English barons forced King John to sign the **Magna Carta**. This document gave certain rights to nobles, merchants, and other English people. It reduced the king's power.

Colonial United States

The original American colonies were a part of Great Britain. In 1775, they went to war with Britain. In 1776, Americans wrote a Declaration of Independence and began the process of becoming a self-governing nation. In 1789, America's leaders wrote the U.S. Constitution. They formed a government in which people elected leaders to represent their wishes. This government was based in part on their knowledge of the British Parliament. It was also based on the way many states were organized.

The U.S. government has three branches. The legislative branch, called Congress, makes the laws. Voters elect members of Congress. Led by a president, the executive branch carries out the laws. The president is elected by the people. The third branch is the judicial branch. It decides what the laws and Constitution mean. The highest court in the judicial branch is the Supreme Court. It has nine judges who are appointed for life by the president.

At the time of the writing of the Constitution, the United States already had a large population. It was not practical to gather all the people together to discuss issues and vote.

1215	English Magna Carta written
1707	British Constitution signed
1776	U.S. Declaration of Independence adopted
1832	U.K. Reform Act approved

KINDS OF DEMOCRACIES

The earliest forms of democracy were direct democracies. People gathered to talk about issues and make decisions. This form of democracy worked well in the beginning. When the U.S. government formed, people met in a New England town hall to solve problems. As the cities and the country began to grow, the issues became bigger. It was difficult for each person to be present at these decision-making meetings.

Not many countries use direct democracy as a form of government, but many community organizations use it. For example, U.S. labor **unions** often meet to discuss issues. They decide issues that relate to the whole group by majority vote.

During labor union meetings, members discuss and vote on important issues such as pay and worker safety.

Referendums

Some countries and states use referendums. A referendum is a proposal for a new law. People vote directly on referendums rather than through their elected leader. In 2004, the leaders of the **European Union** considered having one constitution for all of the member countries. Some countries had their leaders decide. However, in France and Netherlands, a referendum was held. The people voted. They decided they did not want to use the European Union's constitution. The people decided to keep their own.

Representative Democracy

Imagine what would happen if every person was asked to vote on every issue. The people of a large nation would spend all of their time voting. A better choice is to use a representative democracy.

In a representative democracy, the people elect others to make decisions for them. People choose leaders who think and feel the same as they do to make decisions for them. The elected leaders have many responsibilities, from writing laws to managing programs. For example, the leaders may decide how much money to give to an education program. They might make rules to make sure businesses run fairly.

A representative democracy has strengths and weaknesses. People are busy working and often taking care of their families. In contrast, leaders have time to study problems. Their job is to debate issues and to reach an agreement with others on the best way to solve problems. However, unless people pay attention, they may not know all the decisions that their leaders have made.

Ideally, leaders represent the beliefs of the people who vote for them. Some leaders consider their own needs and opinions instead of those of the people who vote for them. For this reason, many democracies require leaders to serve short terms, such as two or four years.

In a representative government such as Turkey's, elected officials must please the people who voted for them if they hope to be re-elected.

In a parliamentary form of democracy, the people elect leaders to be part of a parliament. The leaders come from different political parties. Political parties are groups of people who share the same beliefs. When a parliament is formed, one party usually has more leaders, or members, than another. That party becomes the governing party. The head of that party is chosen as the leader of the country, often called the prime minister. The prime minister also appoints other government leaders.

Sometimes one party may have just a few more leaders elected than other parties. It may not have a large majority. What happens then? A smaller party can combine with another party to block the majority. The majority party then has less power. Sometimes this situation forces parliament members to compromise and work together more. Sometimes it causes more disagreements among them. If so, the other members of parliament may call for a new election.

The British Parliament consists of the House of Lords and the House of Commons.

British Parliament

Britain has a Parliament made up of two houses. The House of Lords has lords and ladies. Some **inherited** their position from their family. The government or the Church of England appoints others. Voters elect members of the House of Commons. The prime minister is selected from the majority party in the House of Commons. In modern Britain, the House of Lords has little power. However, it often suggests changes and offers its opinions on laws being considered.

Presidential Democracy

Another form of representative democracy is a presidential democracy. The people elect a president as head of state. The president then chooses people to lead government departments. The people also elect leaders to serve in a legislative body. This body may be a parliament, legislature, or congress. Unlike a parliamentary democracy, the head of state and the legislative body are separated. They often work together to solve problems.

In a presidential democracy, the legislative body discusses and votes on laws. The president has the right to veto a law, or send it back to the legislature to be reconsidered. The legislature may change the law and give it back to the president. They may decide to abandon the law. They may vote on the law again and approve it with enough votes to override the president's veto. This situation rarely occurs because it requires more votes than to merely pass the law.

A president may sign a law or veto a law. When a president vetoes a law, it is sent back to the legislative body for reconsideration.

RIGHTS OF THE PEOPLE

Would a democracy work if people could not vote? What if they were not allowed to meet in public? What if they could not disagree with their leaders? A democracy works only if the people are given rights. These rights are often promised through a constitution and other laws.

People in a democracy have a right to disagree with their government.

Common Rights in a Democracy

- Power lies with the people. The government cannot tell its people what to think and believe. People have the freedom to live how they choose.

- People are allowed to vote. Elections are free and fair.

- People have the freedom to practice their religion.

- People are allowed to practice their own culture and traditions.

- People cannot be placed in jail without a reason. They must be given a quick and fair trial.

- People in a democracy are allowed to express themselves. They can say and write what they want.

- People have the right to assemble, or gather. They can gather in groups to discuss problems. They are allowed to form groups, such as unions or political parties.

- People should be treated equally. Each person's vote and opinion should count the same.

In a democracy, citizens vote privately so no one can see their decision.

Tax money helps the government provide highways, firefighters, teachers, and other services that benefit all the people.

Responsibilities of the People

With rights come responsibilities. In a democracy, people must respect the rights of others. Citizens must be tolerant of others who practice religions that are different from their own. They must allow people to have different cultural beliefs. They must allow people to have different ideas.

People have the right to believe and work as they see fit. But a nation cannot allow people to work in ways that are dangerous to other people. For example, they cannot risk other people's lives. So nations have the right to create laws. People who do not follow these laws receive punishments, such as fines or jail time. A democracy does not work if people do not respect the laws.

Everyone in a community benefits from police and roads. Laws require people to pay taxes, which support these services. People must also recognize that they are part of a bigger democratic state with many differing viewpoints. There are times when it is necessary to compromise with others.

The people in a democracy have a right to vote. Along with this right comes the responsibility to exercise this right. People should spend time understanding the issues to make good decisions.

Right to Vote

Those allowed to vote varies according to the nation. Some nations say that people must be a certain age to vote. Others say that only men can vote.

460 BCE In Athens, Greece, only adult men are allowed to vote.

1832 British men who own land are given the right to vote.

1893 In New Zealand, women gain the right to vote.

1920 In the United States, women gain the right to vote.

1994 In South Africa, all people regardless of race are allowed to vote.

In a democracy, people participate by voting. When people read about issues and talk to others about them, they better understand their country's problems. They can share their ideas about how the problems can be solved. They can choose leaders who share their thoughts and beliefs.

Personal Political Acts

People can also take part in organizations that share their opinions and interests. They may join a political party. They may also join other groups. It might be a teacher's union, a group of business owners, a students' group, or a group for senior citizens. Together, they can make sure that issues important to them get the attention of their leaders.

In addition, people can take part by becoming leaders of their local or national government. They may participate in a political campaign or party. They may attend a public debate or community meeting on a topic. They may even hold a protest or start a petition about an issue they care about.

Leaders of the People

In democracies, leaders rise from among the people. For example, Nelson Mandela grew up in South Africa during a time when blacks had few rights. Members of the government had to be white. Mandela helped form the Youth League of the African National Congress in 1944. He was put in jail in 1964. While there, he continued to protest. He urged the whites-only government to hold free elections for all races. He received the **Nobel Peace Prize** for guiding South Africa's peaceful change to free elections for all.

In a democracy, people have a responsibility to participate in public life.

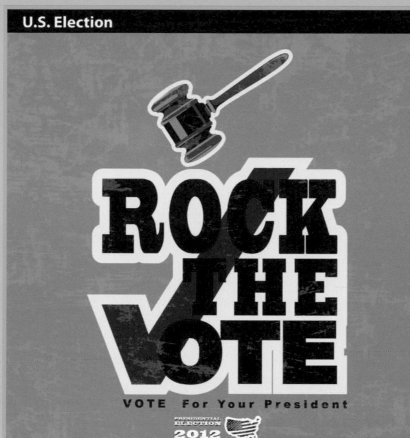

ROCK THE VOTE

VOTE For Your President

PRESIDENTIAL ELECTION
2012

Organizations such as Rock the Vote link voting to political decisions that affect people's lives.

In 1990, a number of musicians banded together to form Rock the Vote. This group for youths encourages young people to become involved in politics. Using music, technology, and popular culture, the group has **registered** over five million youths to vote. Rock the Vote appeals to youths through many celebrity spokespeople, including Lady Gaga, Christina Aguilera, and Justin Timberlake.

Political Parties

Political parties are groups that share similar ideas about government. They help promote candidates who represent their viewpoints. They may sponsor debates and make commercials. In this way, political parties help people understand a candidate's ideas. Some nations, such as the United States, Canada, and the United Kingdom, have two main parties. Other nations, such as France, Germany, Israel, and South Africa, have multiparty systems.

POWER GRAB

Governments decide many things. They decide who pays taxes. They control education. They also determine who serves in the military and who can vote. They oversee a wide variety of workers and community services. Services provided by the government include schools, parks, police, the military, and museums.

In a democracy, the people make the decisions that shape how the government is run. This means that even when elected leaders run government, the people are still the source of power. The people have the power because they decide who those elected leaders will be.

Voters hold their leaders accountable for their decisions.

The Leaders' Choices

The executive and legislative leaders work with the permission of the people. Some leaders think their job is to vote the way that the people who elected them request. They will often do surveys to see what people think. Then they vote based on those decisions. Others vote based on their own thoughts and beliefs.

Sometimes leaders may vote for a policy even when they think it is a bad idea. They do this to try to please the people who elected them. Other times, leaders may ignore what the people want.

Adolf Hitler

In 1933, the Nazi party had control of the German parliament. Nazis chose Adolf Hitler as the **chancellor**. The parliament then passed laws that allowed Hitler to ignore the constitution and increase his power. The president of Germany died. Hitler took over his job as well. As Hitler increased his power, the power of the people decreased.

Democracies encourage transparency. They try to do their work in a way that the people know what was discussed and what decisions were made.

Protecting the People's Power

In a democracy, leaders generally serve short terms. Elections are held often. This gives people the chance to remove leaders who are making decisions they do not agree with.

The length of term a leader serves depends on the nation and its laws. Leaders cannot extend their time in leadership unless people vote for them again. This keeps a person from staying in office permanently and gathering more power than allowed.

Most democracies also have laws that encourage transparency. Transparency means that most of the work of the leaders happens in public. Members of the media and other people can watch their work and report their actions to the public.

Most democracies are set up to separate the different branches of the government. For example, the courts are separate from the lawmaking groups. This system keeps one group or one person from having too much power.

In a modern society, people cannot make all decisions for a government. Citizens are too many, too widely spread, and too busy. People elect leaders to represent them instead.

Leaders of the legislative branch make the laws. This group may be called a congress or parliament. They discuss and reach decisions on issues.

Some nations have a separate executive branch that is responsible for making sure the laws are carried out. It is also in charge of the day-to-day running of the nation. The executive branch may be led by a president, prime minister, or chancellor. These people may appoint other leaders to help carry out their work.

Finally, the judicial branch is responsible for making sure the laws are enforced. The leaders of this branch are judges. There may be many different levels of judges, from Supreme Court justices to local judges.

Judges interpret the meaning of the laws. They make sure the laws are applied fairly.

The Citizens in Power

All of the leaders are guided by a constitution. This document explains their responsibilities. It also sets their limits. For example, it tells who is responsible for government services and organizations.

Ultimately, the citizens are in charge. If they are displeased with the actions or beliefs of the elected leaders, they will not vote them back into power.

Sir Winston Churchill served as the British prime minister during World War II. Before that, he served as a leader in several other roles in government. As prime minister, he helped lead Britain through the war with his strategies and his speeches. He helped inspire people in Britain and around the world.

Kim Dae Jung was a leader in South Korea's National Assembly in 1961. Just weeks after being elected, the democracy was overthrown. He worked for years to restore the democracy. There were several attempts to kill him. He was placed in prison for many years without a trial. In 1997, he was elected president. He worked to reform the government throughout his term. In 2000, he was awarded the Nobel Peace Prize.

When people go to vote, they may be asked to sign a form. Sometimes they must show that they registered to vote. They may be given a special code to enter into the voting machine. Then they are allowed to vote in private. Why are all of these **safeguards** taken?

People are not charged a fee or tax to vote. In some places, a poll tax was once charged. Its goal was to keep poor people and other groups from voting.

People also have a right to vote without being bullied. Special observers make sure that people feel safe in voting for whom they choose. They provide a safe place. They let people vote in secret so no one can hurt them for choosing their candidate.

Safeguarding Democracy

In a democracy, it is important that an election be free and fair. Several safeguards make sure this happens. In a democracy, officials take care to make sure that every vote is made freely and every vote counts. Special observers watch the elections. They make sure that there is no cheating in the voting process. They may check to make sure that people are eligible to vote in the election.

Keeping Elections Free and Fair

International groups often work together to help organize elections. They serve as special observers for the elections. For example, in 2012, Sierra Leone held democratic elections after years of civil war. Teams of observers from the European Union were invited to watch the elections. They made sure the elections were free and fair.

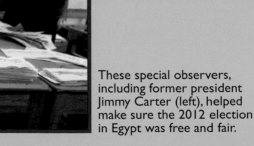

These special observers, including former president Jimmy Carter (left), helped make sure the 2012 election in Egypt was free and fair.

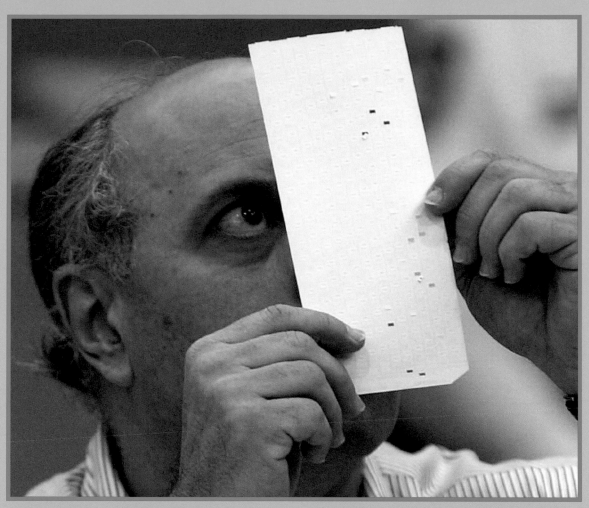

After the 2000 U.S. election, officials in some Florida counties had to examine individual ballots. They checked which candidate was chosen.

Campaigning Candidates

Another group works to make sure that all candidates are treated the same. This group stays neutral. It may have members from all the parties involved. Working with several political parties helps make sure that no single candidate is getting special treatment. They watch the political **campaigns**, the voting, and the counting of votes. They also settle any complaints or disputes.

Sometimes election results are uncertain, and independent groups must examine the votes. For example, in the 2000 U.S. election, George W. Bush ran against Al Gore. Problems with the voting in Florida arose. Gore asked that the votes be recounted. A state group recounted the votes. Gore disagreed with the findings. The Supreme Court finally determined that Bush was the winner of the election.

National Powers

Many democracies divide the government into different areas. The national government can look very different in different nations. Some leave most of the control at the local level, such as in county or city government. The national government is not very involved. Other democracies have a stronger national government system.

The national government is responsible for collecting national taxes. It decides how to use the tax money. It is also in charge of directing the military. It decides who serves, where they serve, and what they do. The national government also handles relationships with other nations. It might make agreements with other countries. It watches over trade with other nations to make sure business on both sides is fair.

National governments are in charge of printing currency.

Regional and Local Powers

Would it make sense for the national government to decide where to place a new street sign? What about how many police officers are needed in a certain city? These kinds of issues are left to regional and local powers.

The structure of a regional government may vary from one region to another within a nation. Regions may be areas such as a province, territory, or state. Each region may have its own constitution to guide its leaders.

A local government might include a city, township, or county. These local governments are responsible for issues in that specific area. They take care of many of the issues of daily life. They are responsible for many public safety services, such as fire departments, police departments, emergency medical services, and traffic control. Many times, the three levels of government share similar interests and work together.

Some issues that affect only people in a small area, such as traffic and safety, are best handled at the local level.

Education in the United States

Education is an example of how power is divided and shared among national, regional, and local governments. The national Department of Education in the United States makes sure that education is for all students.
The state departments of education help select textbooks. They decide what subjects the children in their states must learn. The local school boards decide how the material is taught.

THE LAW

Laws are important in a democracy because they protect the rights of the people. They also limit the power of the government. The laws show the wishes of the majority of the people. However, a constitution often helps make sure that the rights of small groups are protected.

The Constitution Rules

A constitution is a set of rules and shared beliefs for a nation. It explains the rights and responsibilities of the people and their leaders. A constitution includes such rules as who is allowed to vote and how the government is organized. It may specify when leaders are to be elected and how long they may serve. Most importantly, the constitution specifies the freedoms that must be protected.

Legislators often have help reviewing proposed laws because of their length. The 2010 Affordable Care Act is more than 2,400 pages long.

For a democracy to work, rules must be enforced. People should be treated fairly and equally.

Lower and Higher

In modern democracies, the court system usually consists of different levels. Different courts are in charge of hearing different types of cases. Lower courts may hear such cases as traffic tickets or **shoplifting**. Higher courts may hear cases involving international business disputes. The highest court, often called a Supreme Court, deals with cases involving constitutional rights.

The Courts

The courts enforce the laws. They are written to treat everyone fairly and equally. All people must be treated the same in the courts. No one is above the law. Everyone should be equally punished if they do not follow these rules. Even the president and elected officials are held to the same rules.

Under many laws, no one can be arrested or put in prison without a reason. People must be told the reason they are being put in jail. In a democracy, people have the right to a fair and quick trial. In addition, the trial cannot be done in secret. It must be done in public. This openness allows others to make sure the trial is fair. The courts must be separate from the other bodies of government. Leaders cannot tell the court what to do in a court case.

BUSINESS MATTERS

What would happen if a government controlled media such as television and the Internet? A government could limit what information the people get. It could keep its activities secret. What happens if the government controls the nation's natural resources? It could limit the people's access to them. It could decide how much people will pay for water or gas. It could decide who gets these resources. People need water. They need power to heat their homes and do their work. People might be afraid to protest to the government because they might lose access to these important resources.

Government Control of Commerce

Even in a democracy, governments are involved with businesses. The government may make rules that keep businesses safe and fair.

For example, the government may say that children may not work in factories or that workers must be given safety gear. The government may form groups that watch for cheating. For example, some companies might try to claim their foods are **organic** when they are not. The government also sets standards for companies to reduce pollution. Its agencies make sure companies meet these standards.

The government may tax businesses. It may also stop a business from buying from or selling to certain nations.

The more dependent people are on the government, the more difficult it is for them to protest.

Special Interests

Some people criticize the democratic process. They say that it is not always fair. They claim that wealthy people and companies have a louder voice. Companies can use their money to influence elected leaders.

Some companies use lobbyists. These people are paid to talk to leaders. They try to persuade them to vote a certain way. For example, imagine that the government uses one company to build planes for its air force. Then the government considers a switch to another group. The original company could hire a lobbyist. The lobbyist would meet with leaders and try to change their minds.

Special interest groups also try to influence leaders. These groups of people share a common interest. They might be senior citizens, autoworkers, or people concerned about animal rights. They work together to try to get leaders to consider their views and beliefs. In this way, the voices of a minority group can be heard. Gathering together in a group gives them a louder voice.

The British Parliament is known as a place where anyone can bring their concerns to members of Parliament. This is where the term *lobbyist* began.

The Revolving Door

Leaders sometimes leave the government and are immediately hired by lobbying groups. Because they know government officials, they become powerful advocates for the group. Sometimes the reverse is also true. Former lobbyists work for the government on issues they once lobbied about. This practice is known as "the revolving door." Some governments are issuing new rules. They require a break of one or more years before a government employee can be hired by a lobbying group.

In the Media

Media includes print resources, such as newspapers, books, and campaign literature. It also includes online sources, such as blogs. In a democracy, people can listen to the radio or watch television to learn about issues. Today, people have access to a great deal of information.

The Media's Role

An important job of the media is to inform the people. The media can serve as a balanced source of information on different issues. It shares a variety of opinions with the people. Many news sources strive to be fair. Still it is important for people to consider whether the information is someone's opinion or a fair explanation of events and ideas.

Another important job of media is to serve as a watchdog. The media can look at leaders' claims to see whether they are truthful. They can alert the public to any lies or unfair actions. The media gives a voice to the poor and to minorities that may not be heard.

The media holds the elected leaders accountable for their decisions.

Stephen Harper became Canada's prime minister in 2006. Leaders in democracies often speak to the media during press conferences to keep the public updated on issues.

Debating the Issues

Another important job of the media is to provide a place for debate. For example, the news media may host a debate. This lets the people hear several people's differing beliefs. The media can also publish editorials. In these opinion pieces, editors explain their beliefs on an issue. The editors may then publish other people's opinions on the topic in letters to the editor.

While the media try to remain fair, the media at times "sets the agenda" by bringing up important issues. Sometimes they purposely highlight a particular issue, question, or decision. Thousands of activities occur in a democracy on any day, from court decisions to committee meetings. Media cannot cover every story, every issue, and every candidate. By choosing which to cover and which to ignore, media plays an important role in how the people are informed.

Media Today

People today have lots of sources of information. With that information comes the responsibility to make informed decisions. News media are not required to be responsible or honest. Some news items are more for entertainment than for information. Citizens must make decisions and choices about the information they get.

ROLE OF CULTURES

People's culture influences their decisions. Many cultures share values such as honesty. These shared values help shape the laws that are made.

Culture Clashes

While many cultures share values, they also differ on certain issues. They may disagree on religious beliefs, how to raise children, or how to dress appropriately. For a democracy to work well, people need to respect each other's differences and still work toward common goals.

The government can play a role in helping to resolve these differences. For example, some cultures have different views on the role of women. Some of them believe that women should not be able to vote. This belief conflicts with other cultures that believe women should have equal rights. The government can help resolve this conflict by establishing rules about the rights of women.

Majority Rule

Majority rule seems like a fair way to make decisions. Each person has a vote. However, at times, powerful people may unfairly influence voters' decisions. For example, a television station could report information about an issue in a way that tries to influence people to vote a certain way. A large business could try to convince its workers to vote for a specific candidate. It might threaten to lay off workers if its candidate is not elected.

Some Muslim cultures require women to cover their faces. France recently passed a law banning veils that conceal a woman's face. The law has caused controversy in different French groups.

People across the world can learn about the practices in other countries through television, the Internet, and other media.

Democratic Influences

During the 1900s, several nations switched to a democratic form of government. Part of the reason for this switch is that technology has made media available to many more people. This allowed information to be shared across the world. With this shared information comes a greater understanding of different cultures and governments. As people understand the cultures, they may change their views and practices.

In recent years, many changes have occurred in governments around the world. During the 1990s, the **Soviet Union** collapsed. Several former Soviet nations became democracies. During the 1990s, many forms of government also changed in parts of Africa, including in South Africa and Tunisia. Both countries moved toward more democratic forms of government.

Forms of Government

	Democracy	Dictatorship
Basis of power	People elect officials to represent their views and beliefs.	The dictator controls everything in the country. His word is the law.
Rights of people	People have many rights, including the right to fair and free elections, the right to assemble, and the right to choose how to live their lives.	The people have very few rights. Their duty is to do whatever the dictator wants.
How leaders are chosen	Frequent and regular elections are held to vote for leaders.	Leaders can inherit their position or take it with military force. The most powerful political party may also choose them.
Basis of judicial branch	A separate judicial branch enforces the laws made by the legislative branch. Laws are supposed to be enforced freely and fairly.	The judicial branch does what the dictator wants.
Relation of business to the form of government	Government plays a limited role in businesses. They may charge taxes and make some laws to make sure businesses are run fairly.	The government often owns the major businesses in a country.
Control of media	The government does not control the media. People have access to many opinions and diverse information from the media.	The dictator either tells the media what to report or **censors** the media's reports.
Role of religion	People may choose to practice their own religion.	People may or may not be able to practice their religion freely. However, political parties and focus on the dictator's personality are more important than religion.

Monarchy	Oligarchy	Theocracy
A monarch's power is inherited from a previous **generation.** In absolute monarchies, monarchs are believed to be chosen by God.	A select few use their wealth or connections to powerful people in the government to rule. They are rarely elected.	The government is based on the state religion.
Rights are not guaranteed in an **absolute monarchy**. In a **constitutional monarchy**, rights are outlined in the country's constitution.	No rights are guaranteed, but in elected oligarchies, citizens can vote.	The laws of the state religion limit the rights of the people.
Power is passed down through families. Monarchies have different rules for who inherits power. In constitutional monarchies, the leaders of governing bodies, such as a parliament, are chosen through elections.	Oligarchs take power in most cases. They are rarely elected. They usually lead hidden behind the government.	Leaders are elected or appointed or chosen by religious customs.
In absolute monarchies, monarchs run the courts. Most constitutional monarchies have a separate judicial branch to ensure fair treatment.	Most oligarchies hide behind regular government functions. With their money and power, they affect the judicial branch's decisions.	All laws are based on the state religion. The judicial branch bases its judgments on that religion's laws.
Leaders of absolute monarchies control all of the wealth of a country. In constitutional monarchies, decisions about business are made by a governing body, such as a parliament.	Many oligarchs control wealthy businesses.	Businesses can be owned by citizens or by the government.
The press is not free in an absolute monarchy. Many constitutional monarchies, however, guarantee freedom of the media and speech.	Oligarchs tend to own and control all the media.	The media can be controlled by the government or by private citizens. It must follow the laws of the state religion.
Absolute monarchies often require people to have the same religion as the monarch. Many constitutional monarchies guarantee freedom of religion.	Some oligarchs share a common religion.	Religion forms the basis of the government. It dictates most aspects of the citizens' lives.

ASSESSING DEMOCRACY

Here are some of the advantages of a democracy.

- The people in a democratic form of government have the power. The leaders must listen to the beliefs and opinions of the people. This process may make the people feel more satisfied with the government.

- Because people have input into their government, they are inspired to defend their nation.

- The people in a democracy have basic rights. They enjoy a wide range of personal freedoms.

- Because a democratic form of government relies on a majority, leaders must cooperate. Hearing other's opinions and reasons as they try to find agreement leads to better decisions.

- If leaders are taking too much power or abusing their positions, they will not be re-elected. These changes can be made without any violence. This peaceful process prevents civil wars that are more common with other forms of government.

In a democracy, people's personal freedoms include the freedom to choose where they want to live and work.

It can be difficult for a democratic government to act quickly on urgent issues.

Democracy's Disadvantages

While democracy has many advantages, there are some disadvantages.

- Since the leaders are representing the people, they may place more **emphasis** on opinions than on knowledge. The leaders in a democracy must keep the people happy. This pressure can make it difficult for the leaders to make decisions. They may choose to vote for a law or policy they do not believe in just to keep the voters happy.

- Because the leaders are in office for a short period of time, the policies of democratic forms of government can suffer from short-term thinking. A leader may start a program or work toward a goal, but the new leaders may not agree with this program.

- In a democracy, many people are needed to make decisions. Getting that many people to agree can take a long time. Therefore, in a democratic form of government, it can take longer to make decisions.

- A democracy functions best when its people are educated. Not every citizen takes the time or effort to keep informed of the decisions and discussions of their leaders.

- In majority rule, the majority makes the policies. A group of leaders may be in the majority and use its power to make rules that hurt a minority. For example, many years ago, all members of the U.S. Congress were men. They made rules saying that women could not vote.

POWER OF THE PEOPLE

Democracies differ from other forms of government because the power lies with the people. The people either vote for laws directly, or they elect leaders to represent them.

Democratic forms of government have several advantages. They encourage the input of the people. They limit the abuse of power by leaders. They also have disadvantages, including short-term thinking and the difficulty to respond quickly to issues as they arise.

For the People

Shared beliefs are the core of democracies. These governments are built around a constitution. The constitution protects the rights of the people.

People in democracies have many more rights and freedoms than people have in other forms of government. Some of these freedoms include the freedom to assemble, express themselves, practice religion, and have free and fair elections.

The U.S. Constitution explains the shared beliefs of the people and how government should be organized.

In a democracy, people can gather freely and express their opinions.

By the People

The number of democratic forms of government has increased over the years. At the same time, the problems of individual nations have become international issues.

Changing nations face new problems. One issue facing these nations is the question of whether a nation's people can freely choose democracy. For example, if a nation's people have been fighting each other, is it right for other democratic nations to interfere? Should they step in and help set up a democratic form of government?

As nations cooperate to support other nations, big decisions must be made. Some nations believe that democratic nations should encourage other nations to use democracy. For example, in 2001, Afghans defeated their religious **dictatorship**. Afghanistan needed a new government. A group of nations tried to start a democracy within Afghanistan.

Arab Spring

During the 2010s, several countries in the Middle East changed their form of government from dictatorships to democracies because of protests by their citizens. These uprisings became known as the Arab Spring. Sometimes this switch has led to such violence and **chaos** that other countries have become involved.

Democracies on the international level must also look at how they can work together. There is a big imbalance between wealthier democracies and less developed democracies. Democratic nations around the world must decide what responsibilities they have toward each other.

Documents of Democracy

Preamble to the U.S. Constitution (1787)

"We the People of the United States, in Order to form a more perfect Union, establish Justice, insure domestic Tranquility, provide for the common defence, promote the general Welfare, and secure the Blessings of Liberty to ourselves and our **Posterity**, do ordain and establish this Constitution for the United States of America."

Magna Carta (1215)

Written in the 1200s, the Magna Carta was an agreement between a group of English barons and King John. The barons wanted new protections for their lands and money, and changes to various laws. The king agreed to the barons' demands to avoid a civil war. Just ten weeks after the Magna Carta was signed, however, the nation plunged into civil war.

The Magna Carta contains a preamble and 63 clauses. Two clauses are given below.

Section 39

"No free man shall be arrested or imprisoned or **disseised** or outlawed or exiled or in any way victimised, neither will we attack him or send anyone to attack him, except by the lawful judgment of his peers or by the law of the land.

Section 61

"Since, moreover, for God and the betterment of our kingdom and for the better **allaying** of the discord that has arisen between us and our barons we have granted all these things aforesaid, wishing them to enjoy the use of them **unimpaired** and unshaken for ever, we give and grant them the under-written security."

Canadian Charter of Rights and Freedoms (1982)

Guarantee of Rights and Freedoms

"1. The *Canadian Charter of Rights and Freedoms* guarantees the rights and freedoms set out in it subject only to such reasonable limits prescribed by law as can be **demonstrably** justified in a free and democratic society.

Fundamental Freedoms

"2. Everyone has the following fundamental freedoms:

- (a) freedom of **conscience** and religion;
- (b) freedom of thought, belief, opinion and expression, including freedom of the press and other media of communication;
- (c) freedom of peaceful assembly; and
- (d) freedom of **association**.

GLOSSARY

absolute monarchy A government in which a ruler controls every aspect of government. Rule is passed along family lines.

agenda A list of items to be considered in a meeting

allaying Relieving, calming

association The act of having friends, partners, or companions

blogs Websites that consist of online personal journals with comments on public and private issues

campaigns Connected series of actions designed to bring about a specific result. For example, political campaigns are designed to get a candidate elected.

censors Prevents publication or deletes ideas that cause offense or go against the government's views and goals

chambers Legislatures or other groups of lawmakers. Also known as houses.

chancellor A high official or head of government. Sometimes a prime minister is called a chancellor.

chaos Complete confusion, disorder

communes The smallest districts of government of many countries, especially in Europe

conscience The knowledge of right and wrong and the feeling that someone should do what is right

consensus General agreement

constitution A document containing the basic beliefs and laws of a nation, state, or social group. Constitutions establish the powers and duties of the government and guarantee certain rights to the people.

constitutional monarchy A monarchy in which the powers of the ruler are restricted to the powers that are stated in the constitution and laws of the nation

demonstrably Able to be proven or shown

dictatorship A system of government in which the leader of a country has absolute power

disseised To have one's land or possessions wrongfully taken away

emphasis Special importance

European Union Economic, scientific, and political organization consisting of 27 countries in Europe

generation Individuals who are one step in the line of a descent of a family. A grandmother, mother, and daughter are three generations of a family.

inherited Received something by legal right from a person when that person died

legislature An organized group of people elected to make or pass laws

lottery A random drawing of names from a large group

Magna Carta A document that gave specific rights to the English people

Nobel Peace Prize An important award given to individuals or organizations around the world to honor their work in promoting peace

oligarchy A government in which a small group exercises control. Wealth and power is concentrated in just a few people's hands.

organic Describes food grown without the use of laboratory-made fertilizers, growth substances, antibiotics, or pesticides

parliament A group of people who have the duty and power to make the laws of a country

participate To take part in

posterity Future generations

registered Written in a list or record; proved to be legally able to vote

safeguards Things that protect

shoplifting Stealing from a store

Soviet Union Also known as the Union of Soviet Socialist Republics, a country formed of 15 now-independent republics

unimpaired Perfect; not damaged

unions Groups of workers joined together to protect their wages and benefits and improve their working conditions

FOR MORE INFORMATION

Books

Christelow, Eileen. *Vote!* New York: Sandpiper, 2008.

Fitzpatrick, Anne. *Democracy*, Forms of Government. Mankato, MN: The Creative Company, 2007.

Grodin, Elissa. *D Is for Democracy: A Citizen's Alphabet.* Ann Arbor, MI: Sleeping Bear Press, 2007.

O'Donnell, Liam. *Democracy*, Cartoon Nation. North Mankato, MN: Capstone Press, 2008.

Woolf, Alex. *Democracy*, Systems of Government. Milwaukee, WI: World Almanac Library, 2006.

Websites

Ben's Guide to U.S. Government for Kids: bensguide.gpo.gov/3-5/index.html

Democracy Kids: www.democracykids.org/demo_kids_1/main.swf

Congress for Kids: www.congressforkids.net/Independence_democracy.htm

Kidipede—History and Science for Kids: www.historyforkids.org/learn/government/democracy.htm

iCivics: www.icivics.org

INDEX